Epsilon Pr

Pres

Skin Tight

by
Gary Henderson

Cast and Crew

Elizabeth	Angela Bull
Tom	John Schumacher

Director	Jemma Gross
Designer	Jessamy Willson-Pepper
Lighting Designer	Sherry Coenen
Stage Manager	Anna Robertson
Composer and Sound Designer	Gareth Jones
Fight Director	Dan Styles
Movement Director	Clare McKenna
Production Photographer	Andy Colbourne
Art Designer	Al Stride
Projection Designer	Grant Kay
Associate Artists	Holly Mapels
	William Hartley
	Sarah Bradnum

Epsilon Productions bring SKIN TIGHT to Park Theatre, London after a UK tour during the summer of 2012 for which the production gained critical acclaim.

www.epsilonproductions.co.uk

Epsilon Productions would like to dedicate this production of SKIN TIGHT at Park Theatre to George and Margaret Bull.

Gary Henderson

Skin Tight

B L O O M S B U R Y

LONDON · NEW DELHI · NEW YORK · SYDNEY

Bloomsbury Methuen Drama

An imprint of Bloomsbury Publishing Plc

50 Bedford Square	1385 Broadway
London	New York
WC1B 3DP	NY 10018
UK	USA

www.bloomsbury.com

Bloomsbury is a registered trade mark of Bloomsbury Publishing Plc

First published by Playmarket 2007

First published by Bloomsbury Methuen Drama 2013

© Gary Henderson 2007, 2013

All photographs in the publication by Andy Colbourne

British Library Cataloguing-in-Publication Data
A catalogue record for this book is available from the British Library.

ISBN: PB: 978-1-4725-3201-5
ePDF: 978-1-4725-2896-4
ePub: 978-1-4725-2594-9

Library of Congress Cataloging-in-Publication Data
A catalog record for this book is available from the Library of Congress.

Typeset by Mark Heslington Ltd, Scarborough, North Yorkshire
Printed and bound in Great Britain

Director's Note

Inspired by Denis Glover's heart-breaking poem 'The Magpies', Skin Tight, to me, is about the universal experience of love and loss, and the constant push and pull of everyday life. This daily tug-of-war we have within ourselves, this fight between our own personal desires and our public duties is a subject I am constantly drawn to. As we are deep within a world recession and a time of global uncertainty, where everyday life is made hard, it can be a struggle to just keep going and relationships fracture under the pressure.

Through Tom and Elizabeth we are fortunate to have a glimpse into the extraordinary passion of this ordinary couple. A couple like any other who have struggled with family pressures and financial burdens; who have been swept along and separated by war and duty; who have fought to survive against acts of Nature to keep their livelihood and their home. Ultimately, they are a couple who had to just keep going but wouldn't have survived it without the other. Perhaps, in the end, the human condition is to be left all alone, but this piece reminds me that the journey is all about companionship. And that the memory of someone, of a moment that no-one else knows, can sustain and nourish us totally.

Angela Bull and John Schumacher

Angela Bull – Elizabeth

Angela has worked extensively throughout her career in many areas of the profession from Motion Capture for X-Box to running her own theatre company and producing plays of critical acclaim.

Theatre credits include: *Twelfth Night* (Salon Collective); *Elegies for Angels, Punks and Raging Queens* (Chrysalis Productions); *Recognition of Shakuntala* (Grit Productions & Community 20); *Hamlet* (Twisted Elbow); *Dragon Variation and Double Double* (BHJ Productions); *Blood Wedding* (CP Theatre Productions); *The Way of the World* (Onatti Theatre Co.); *God* (Birmingham Stage Co); *Sweeney Todd* (Spotlighters).

For Epsilon Productions: *Extremities, Othello* and *Fun like Stalingrad.*

Film credits include: *The Magic Flute* (Kenneth Branagh); *Dom* (More Or Less Productions); British indie flick *3 Stags* (Fort Mark Films); *Taxi-Playing Against the Clock* winner of Best Picture at the Rob Knox Film Festival (Bongo Reef Pictures).

TV appearance includes: *Doctors* and *Dangerfield* (BBCTV).

Radio includes: *Postcards from a Cataclysm* (Radio 4 and The Factory) and a one woman production *The Desk* (Promising Productions).

Angela Bull and John Schumacher

John Schumacher – Tom

Liverpool born, John trained at the Royal Welsh College of Music and Drama.

Theatre credits include: John in *After Miss Julie* (Irish tour); Scullery in *Road* (Piccolo Teatro, Milan); Solinus in *Comedy Of Errors* (Swan, Stratford), Kyle in *Helianthus* (Squat Collective); Dad in *Quadrophenia* (UK number 1 touring production).

For Epsilon Productions: Raul in *Extremities*.

Film credits include: *Violet City* and *Part Vampire*.

Jemma Gross – Director

In 2011 Jemma became a member of the prestigious Lincoln Center Theater's Director's Lab in New York and is a member of the Young Vic Genesis Directors Network. Jemma is also Associate Producer of the So and So Arts Club, an international networking club for artists from all disciplines.

Jemma studied European Drama with French at Sussex University before acting at the London Centre for Theatre Studies with The Actors Company.

Theatre Directing credits: *To Freedom's Cause* (GMDT, UK tour and London); *The Shoemaker's Holiday* (RSC Outdoor Theatre); *Mayor Of Zalamea* (Drama Centre); *Twelfth Night* (Salon Collective, Hoxton Hall); *Giddy Goat* and *Shakespeare for Breakfast* (C Venues, Edinburgh Festival); *100% Comedy 100% Chekhov* (Bridewell Theatre), *The Duchess of Malfi* (White Bear Theatre).

Theatre Assistant Directing credits: *Relatively Speaking* (Dir: Maurice Thorogood, Maxim Teatern Stockholm); *King John* (Dir: Phil Wilmott, Union Theatre – *Time Out* Critics Choice and nominated Best Off West End Production and Best Director 2012); *The Belles Stratagem* (Dir: Jessica Swale, Southwark Playhouse – *Time Out* Critics Choice, Nominated Best Off West End Production 2011).

Follow her blog at *www.jemmagross.com* or on Twitter: @JemmaGross

Jessamy Willson-Pepper – Designer

Jessamy trained at Nottingham Trent University and has been designing set and costume for theatre and Notting Hill Carnival in since 2005.

Theatre credits include: *Scratch* (Skin and Bone); *Chekhov Short's, The Strange Case of Dr Jekyll and Mr Hyde* (European Art Company).

For Epsilon Productions: *Extremities.*

Sherry Coenen – Lighting Designer

Sherry has been lighting shows in the US and UK since graduating with a BFA in Lighting Design from the University of Miami in 2003.

Theatre credits include: *The Cabinet Of Dr Caligari, Moby-Dick, Conquest of the South Pole* (Arcola); *Enter* (Embassy Theatre); *Your Last Breath* (UK tour), *Anton Chekhov* (Hampstead Theatre); *Frobisher's Gold* (Shaw); *Mysterious Skin* (The Drill Hall); *Othello*

(Chelsea Theatre); *Bernarda Alba* (Union); *Where The Flowers Grow* (Warehouse Theatre); *The Shakespeare Conspiracy* (Chelsea Theatre).

Angela Bull and John Schumacher

Anna Robertson – Stage Manager

Anna is a Stage Manager from Glasgow who has worked throughout the UK since graduating from college in 2012. She specialises in managing physical theatre, dance and circus.

Theatre credits include: *The Odd Couple* (Stowaways Theatre); *Mezcla Club Cabaret* (Spinal Chord); *The Birthday Party* (Bright Night International).

Various design and technical roles include: Live Sound Operator – *Jekyll*; Sound Designer – *Titus Andronicus;* Lighting Designer – *42nd Street* and *When The Clown Laughs*; Sound Assistant – *Songs for a New World*.

Gareth Jones – Composer and Sound Design

Gareth graduated from the Royal Welsh College of Music and Drama in 2007 and began working for No Fit State Circus as a musician/performer. He has toured around the world with them with *Tabu* and *Mundo Parellelo*.

2010 saw his first composing job with *Canto* and *6½ Flying Circus*, a flying trapeze piece in which he played live.

Gareth has returned to No Fit State Circus to work on site specific productions *Labyrinth* and *Bianco* for the Eden Project.

Dan Styles – Fight Director

Dan is a skilled fight performer, teacher and co-ordinator in various styles of both armed and unarmed combat. He has choreographed fights on well over 80 productions for stage, screen video games and events.

Theatre credits include: *The Three Musketeers*; *Romeo and Juliet* (three times); *Macbeth*; *Twelfth Night*; *The Taming of the Shrew*; *As You Like It* (twice); *Troilus and Cressida*; *A Clockwork Orange*; *Of Mice and Men*; *Lord of the Flies*; *The Madness of King George*; *Journey's End*; *A View From the Bridge*; *Bugsy Malone*; *A Chorus Line*; *High School Musical*; *Hairspray*; *1001 Nights*; *The Playboy of the Western World*; *The Legend of Beowulf*; *Aladdin* (six times); *Foreskin's Lament*.

Screen credits include: Features – *Tooting Broadway*; *Harsh Light of Day*; *Charlene*; *Fossil*. Short films – *Magnesium*; *The Scourge*; *School Run*; *Hope*; *Hold The Lift*; *Relentless*; *Marlowe*. TV – *Damian*. Music videos – *Corruption*; *Charge*.

www.danstyles.com

Clare McKenna – Movement Director

Clare McKenna trained and worked with Philippe Gaulier in Paris and London.

Movement Director credits include: *The Wild Duck* (BARD Summerscape, New York); *Irish Blood, English Heart* (Trafalgar Studios); *King John* (Union Theatre); *The Roman Bath* (Arcola).

Choreography includes: large chorus groups, stage fights and helping actors through physical character work, for shows such as *A Tale of Two Cities* and *Animal Farm* (Crescent Theatre, Birmingham).

Devising work has taken her to festivals such as the London Mime Festival; the Shanghai International Theatre Festival; the Seville Clown Festival; the Dublin and Edinburgh Fringe, and others.

In 2009 she was one of the first participants to take part in the LAByrinth Theatre Company's Summer Intensive Ensemble, New York and has been returning yearly.

Facilitating work includes: The Almedia; The Old Vic; The Barbican.

www.clare.mckenna.com

Andy Colbourne – Production Photographer

Andy has been Epsilon's official photographer for the last three years. He has won awards for his wildlife photography and has recently shot the album cover for the anticipated debut album for *Roman Remains*.

Angela Bull and John Schumacher

Angela Bull and John Schumacher

Al Stride – Art Designer

Al has been working with images and words for longer than he cares to remember. An associate of Epsilon for several years, he is always keen to lend a Mac to their productions! He dreams of opening a penguin farm in Devon.

alistride@me.com

Epsilon Production List

Othello – 2006

Fun Like Stalingrad – 2007

Extremities – 2011 Nominated for Best Director and
Best Stage Fight Direction – Offies
Best Fringe Production – London Festival Fringe

Special thanks go to

evo° *www.evohair.co.uk*

Online *www.onlinerepro.co.uk*

LIBERTY SHOPFITTERS *www.liberty-shopfitters.co.uk*

John & Leila Davey at the Shaftsbury Tavern, N19

Chris Stiling and Victoria Bacon of
Primrose Hill Framing Company

Catriona and Michael Hudson

Sheila Colbourne

Al Stride

Grant Kay

Kate Stafford

Holly Maples

Sarah Bradnum

William Hartley

Ross Newell

To all who generously donated to our Crowd-Funding site

Angela Bull and John Schumacher

A note about under-reading

I first encountered under-reading from a marvellous teacher and director Brian Astbury. Under-reading is simply not having the actors holding onto a script whilst rehearsing. Instead their lines are fed to them by an 'under-reader' (another actor or person

John Schumacher, Clare McKenna, Dan Styles, Angela Bull, Jemma Gross

Sarah Bradnum, John Schumacher, Angela Bull, William Hartley

in the room). The under-reader shadows them and feeds them their lines in short bursts whilst keeping the sense of the sentence. For actors, you are literally freed from the script. Immediately the focus is on your partner and on your environment. You are allowed to respond instinctively to the text, listening to your gut response. For the director I have found that discoveries of character and text are found sooner, actors make riskier choices quicker, and lose their fear of leaping into the unknown. Excitingly, it allows for exploration of movement, fight and voice work to happen alongside the text as opposed to often coming second in a separate rehearsal. It is a phenomenal way of working that I recommend to everyone!

(For more details on this please see Trusting the Actor by Brian Astbury or Jemma's blog at *www.jemmagross.com*).

About Park Theatre

With two theatres, an education suite, a café bar and a gallery, London's newest venue is fully accessible and pleasantly air-conditioned! So, please make Park Theatre your regular home from home – and visit us again ... and again!

We are very grateful to all the individuals and corporations who have made generous donations to help us meet the costs of building the state-of-the-art theatre complex that you are in today. However, the finances of running a theatre of this scale are such that ticket sales alone cannot cover our costs. With no money from the Arts Council we need support to fund on-going expenditure and enable us to stage high quality productions.

We have launched a number of schemes including becoming a Friend, naming a seat, sponsoring a production and legacy giving. The benefits for donors range from priority booking to corporate entertainment. So, whether you would like to donate as little as ten pounds, fund a complete production or something in between, we would be delighted to hear from you! Thank you,

Jez Bond, Artistic Director

development@parktheatre.co.uk

For Park Theatre

Staff

Artistic Director	Jez Bond
Executive Director	Miranda Bertram
Creative Director	Melli Bond
General Manager	John-Jackson Almond
Administrative Coordinator	Amy Lumsden
Technical Manager	Adam Pritchard
President	Jeremy James

Correct at time of going to print. The staff, however, is growing!

Board

Frances Carlisle
Stephanie Dittmer
Nick Frankfort
Colin Hayfield (Chair)
Rachel Lewis

Skin Tight

To Robin and Rowena Henderson

Original Production

First performed at BATS Theatre, Wellington, New Zealand
10 March 1994
with the following cast and creative team:

Tom: Jed Brophy

Elizabeth: Larissa Matheson

Old Man: Frank Edwards

Directed and designed by Gary Henderson

Lighting and original soundtrack by Chris Ward

Inspired by:
the poems 'The Magpies' by Denis Glover
and 'Baptism by River Water' by Sam Hunt,
and by the strength and vitality of the two original actors.

Characters

Tom, *Pakeha, in the prime of his strength and vitality.*
Elizabeth, *Pakeha, similarly in her prime.*
Old Man *(a brief appearance) Pakeha, in his eighties.*

Author's Note

'Pakeha' describes a white New Zealander, usually born in New
Zealand, of European descent.

*The following shows how the Maori names in the text should be
pronounced. These are not the correct Maori pronunciations, but are
an Anglicised version which Pakeha New Zealanders of that era
would have used.*

Heremaia	*Herra – MY – uh*
Oamaru	*Omma – ROO*
Orari	*Uh – RA – ree*
Pukaki	*PEW – cacky*
Rakaia	*Ruh – KY – uh*
Rangitata	*Ranga – TA - tuh (ranga would have a hard 'g' as in bingo)*
Raukapuka	*Racka – POO – kuh*
Tekapo	*TECKa – poe (poe rhymes with toe)*
Waitaki	*WHY – tacky*

A number of gym mats form a single pad centre stage. Behind them, in the centre, is a metal tub full of water, with fruit floating in it – apples and peaches. At each side of the stage, left and right, is an old metal bucket, in line with the centre of the gym mat pad. The buckets are full of water. One has a cloth in it.

Darkness. Loud, pounding music starts. An instant later the lights snap on to reveal a man and a woman, already in motion, sprinting towards each other from either side of the stage. They are young, dressed in a style reminiscent of the 1940s or 1950s, without being too specific. The woman is wearing a dress which buttons down the front. Her arms are bare. The man has a pair of brown woollen work trousers held up by braces over a singlet. Both are barefoot.

They smack into each other in the centre of the stage, and fight.

The fight is brutal. They punch, kick, slap, slam each other to the ground, and wrestle violently, locked together. They are well-matched, with neither gaining the upper hand for more than a few seconds.

There is a hiatus in the music; the furious, high-volume onslaught gives way to a single deep pulse. At the same instant, the fighters detach and roll away from each other. Panting, sweating, glaring at each other, they move to the buckets and douse their heads with water. They continue to eye each other warily, dangerously.

Suddenly the music and the fighters leap forward again, even more viciously than before. This time the fight is shorter, and ends with the woman overpowering the man, sitting astride him while he is flat on his back. She pulls back her fist to punch, but he spreads his arms in a gesture of surrender. She considers for a long beat, then slowly lowers her fist. The man relaxes under her.

She reaches down and grabs the man by the hair at the back of his head. She lifts his head roughly off the floor, leans forward, and kisses him on the lips, hungrily, luxuriously, passionately.

There is the ringing call of magpies.

The woman leans back, wipes her mouth with the back of her hand and gasps, as if she has just drunk a long draught without breathing. She looks down at the man and laughs. Both of them are out of breath.

The woman eases herself off the man, without standing, and moves back until she is sitting against the metal tub. She dips a hand into the water, picks out a peach and takes a big bite. Chewing, she watches the man, an amused look on her face.

Meanwhile the man has moved to one of the buckets, also laughing under his heavy breathing. He reaches into the bucket and lifts out a knife. He holds one hand out to the woman, inviting her to throw him something. Keeping her eyes on the man all the time, she reaches into the tub behind her and takes an apple. She throws it at him, hard. It smacks into his hand. He slices a piece off with the knife, and lifts knife and apple-slice to his mouth. He takes the piece of apple in his mouth and, still watching the woman, licks the juice off the blade. They watch each other for a beat, both chewing. Then . . .

Elizabeth   I have to go.

Tom   Not yet.

Elizabeth   I should have gone hours ago.

Tom *walks over and sits beside her.*

Tom   Plenty of time yet. All the time in the world.

Elizabeth   Oh . . . Tom.

Tom   What?

A beat.

Elizabeth   Yes, you're right. There's time yet.

Elizabeth *bites into the peach. Juice runs down her chin. She lifts her hand to wipe it away, but he stops her with . . .*

Tom   Ah-ah-ah.

Tom *licks the juice off her chin and throat. It becomes a kiss on the lips. He draws away.* **Elizabeth** *eyes him with amusement and takes another bite from the peach.*

Elizabeth *leaps to her feet, and picks up the bucket that doesn't contain the cloth. She pours its contents into the tub. He recoils from the splash. She plonks the bucket down, inverted, and gestures for him to sit on it. As he does, she fetches the other bucket and sets it down beside him.*

Finally, from behind the tub she fetches a mug of soft soap.

Standing behind him, she pushes his braces of his shoulders, down his arms. She does the same with his singlet. His arms are lightly pinned. She takes the cloth from the bucket and squeezes water over his head, shoulders and chest. He gasps at the cold shock. She takes a handful of soap and water, and smears it over his chin, throat, then shoulders and chest – luxuriously and sensually. She takes his knife and swishes it in the water.

Elizabeth Why do you always eat apples that way?

Tom With a knife?

Elizabeth Yes.

She lifts his chin and lays the sharp edge of the blade against his throat, and there is the sound of a blade scraping on metal.

Tom I like the feel of the blade popping through the tight skin. Slicing through the flesh . . .

She begins to shave him.

. . . I like licking the juice off it.

Elizabeth You've done it ever since school. I can remember you sitting on the steps at playtime with your apple and pocket knife. It seemed to me then such a grown-up thing to do.

Tom Impressed?

Elizabeth I noticed.

Tom That's why I did it.

Elizabeth You were barely aware of me.

Tom   You always wore ribbons.

She hesitates for a beat, then continues.

Elizabeth   Do you remember the first time?

Tom   I saw you?

Elizabeth   No. Our first time.

Tom   I remember.

Elizabeth   What do you remember?

Tom   Being nervous.

Elizabeth   Of what?

Tom   Well . . . doing it. For the first time. It was my first time.

Elizabeth   I know. And mine.

Tom   So I was nervous.

Elizabeth   But of what, exactly? What things were you nervous about?

Tom   The gory details?

Elizabeth   I'm intrigued. It's fascinating.

Tom   All right. Well . . . I was afraid I wouldn't be able to . . . find the place.

Elizabeth   The place?

Tom   On you. Where it went in.

Elizabeth   You must have known that I would know.

Tom   But I felt that I was expected to know all that. I even got out this library book. Some medical thing with lots of diagrams. And fingerprints.

Elizabeth   Did it help?

Tom   It might've done, if we'd had the light on. And you'd been a cross-section line drawing.

Elizabeth   What else were you nervous about?

Tom   Oh . . . getting too excited and –

He makes the sound and gesture of firing a pistol.

Or not getting excited enough. But mainly, just not doing it right, I suppose.

Elizabeth   Do you remember anything else?

Tom   Your smell.

She stops shaving in mid stroke.

Elizabeth   What did I smell like?

A beat.

Tom   Cinnamon.

She is still for a beat, considering, then decides he is genuine. She rinses the knife and continues shaving.

Tom   Were you nervous?

Elizabeth   Of course.

A beat. Shaving.

Tom   Well . . . ?

Elizabeth   I was anxious that it would hurt.

Tom   Did it?

Elizabeth   No.

A short beat.

Perhaps a little. And I was worried that . . . this is silly!

Tom   Go on.

Elizabeth   I was worried that it wouldn't fit.

He grins.

Elizabeth   Till I saw it.

The grin fades.

Elizabeth   And I remember touching you.

Tom   You'd done that before.

Elizabeth   No . . . I mean 'touching' you.

Tom   What was that like?

Elizabeth   Strange. Rather thrilling.

She shaves him in silence.

Elizabeth   What were you thinking while we were actually doing it?

Tom   I was thinking . . . 'We're actually doing it!'

They laugh together.

Elizabeth   So was I!

Another few beats of silence.

Tom? Did you enjoy it the first time?

Tom   No, I didn't. Did you?

Elizabeth   No.

She wipes the remaining soap off him with her dress. He looks up, catching her eye, and she pauses. They stare at each other for a beat, then she finishes briskly, empties the bucket into the tub and places it to one side.

Elizabeth   Did you call Christine?

Tom   Christine?

Elizabeth   Kitty.

Tom   Oh.

Elizabeth   She prefers Christine.

Tom   I called her.

Elizabeth   How did she sound?

Tom   Like she was right next door.

Elizabeth   I wish I could have spoken to her. I'd like to see her before I go.

Tom   I told her that.

She looks at him. There is more to say.

Tom   She'll do what she can.

Elizabeth *flings herself down on the floor, on her back, arms outstretched.*

Tom   It's hard for her, Elizabeth.

Elizabeth   I always knew this would happen. I told her –

Tom   Sshh.

Elizabeth   She used to call me her best friend.

Tom   She'll do what she can.

He sits and cuddles her raised knees.

We'll be all right.

Silence.

Elizabeth   What's the time?

Tom   Coming up noon.

Elizabeth   If she gets here in time we should drive out past the farm.

Tom   That'd be a good idea.

Elizabeth   Maybe go down to the swimming hole by the willows. Have a picnic or something. They'd let us, wouldn't they?

Tom   I'm sure they would.

Elizabeth   They know who we are. Anyway, it's our right.

Tom   They'd let us.

Elizabeth   If she gets here in time. Oh, Kitty . . .

Silence. Then he gets to his feet.

Tom   Hey. Remember that time –

Elizabeth   Yes.

Tom   You don't even know what I was going to say.

Elizabeth   I don't have to. I remember everything.

Tom   All right then. What was I going to say?

Elizabeth   I didn't say I knew what you were going to say, I just said that whatever it was that you were going to ask if I remembered I would remember, because I remember everything.

He becomes playful, affecting a strange walk and funny voice.

Tom   All right then. All right, Elizabeth. When we got married, who was the Minister . . .

She is about to answer.

. . . of Agriculture.

She stares at him.

Elizabeth   I only remember important things.

Tom   Ah ha!

Elizabeth   Well I do!

He teases her, pointing his finger, inches from her face. She suddenly leans forward and nips the end of his finger with her teeth. He yelps and rolls away, then springs to his feet.

Tom   How about that time the gang from our class went night swimming down by the willows –

Elizabeth   – down by the willows with kerosene lamps. I remember. We hung the lamps in the trees out over the water.

Tom   It was magical. One of those long South Canterbury summer twilights. It was a good time to be that young.

A beat.

I fell in love with Vicky Pritchard that night.

Elizabeth   Vicky Pritchard?!

Tom   Head over heels for almost a week.

Elizabeth   Pritch the Bitch?!

Tom   She was okay.

Elizabeth   To you perhaps, because you lived over in Raukapuka. You had a farm coming to you. But she never got around with any bottom-end kids in case she caught 'poor germs'. Snob.

Tom   Not everyone in Raukapuka was a snob. I got round with a bottom-end kid.

He crouches behind her and puts his arms around her.

Still do.

Elizabeth   Sometimes I still feel that young.

He grins and places his hands on her breasts.

Tom   I prefer you slightly older.

She firmly removes his hands.

You're not jealous about Vicky Pritchard, are you?

She rolls away to one side, remaining on the floor.

Elizabeth   Of course not. I don't get jealous.

Tom   You do so.

Elizabeth   Me! Jealous! Of what?

Tom   Well . . . me going out with my mates, for instance.

Elizabeth   When did I ever get jealous of you going out with your mates? For instance?

Tom   Oh . . . when we went to the races.

Elizabeth   Nonsense.

Tom Oh yes you did. That time we went up to Addington for the cup. The year Cardigan Bay won it.

He stands with his back to her. She grabs his ankles. During the following exchange he walks across the stage dragging her on the floor behind him, as if she's trying to hold him back.

Tom 'Bye, dear,' I said. And you said –

Elizabeth 'So you're off then.'

Tom And I said, 'Yes. Everything's all right, isn't it?' And you said –

Elizabeth 'Oh yes, fine, fine. You go off and have a wonderful time with the boys.'

Tom And I said, 'You're sure you wouldn't like to come?' And you said –

Elizabeth 'No, no. I'll be fine here. By myself!'

Tom That was jealous.

Elizabeth It was not.

He laughs.

Tom It was.

Elizabeth It was not.

On the word 'not' she strikes at him. He blocks the blow. There is a short fight, where they rain blows on each other, but none land – all are neatly blocked. Finally, she seems to gain the upper hand, but he lands a blow on her face and she spins away. She dips her hand in the tub and puts water on her face.

Elizabeth I hate it when you win.

Tom Then don't turn everything into a matter of winning or losing.

He sits on the floor.

Elizabeth   Some things are. I nearly lost you once because you were trying to win something.

Tom   What?

Elizabeth   The war.

He doesn't want to talk about it.

You left me.

Tom   That wasn't leaving you.

Elizabeth   Oh really? The call came and off you went. Couldn't wait. The big boys' adventure.

Tom   Elizabeth, do we have to? Now?

Elizabeth   Yes. We do. What a waste. What a stupid, stupid waste.

She sits, back to back with him, leaning against him.

You went to war. All of you. All our beautiful boys. Out at Orari Station, leaning out the carriage windows. The Heremaia boys who used to tease me at school, all jammed into one window, yelling, big fat grins on their faces.

Tom   Don't.

Elizabeth   And Gordon Douglas who played on the wing –

Tom   Elizabeth.

Elizabeth   And Lofty Allen with his big bony wrists sticking out the sleeves of his tunic. Like a boy with man's arms. And you. All of you. All our beautiful, indestructible boys, laughing in the sunlight. And we were utterly deceived, cheering and waving and weeping as the train pulled out. Except Mrs Heremaia. Back against the station wall in the shadows. Face like a rock. She knew. But the rest of us – the sunlight on Orari Station deceived us all.

And the telegrams started to come before you'd even had time to get over there. Every day someone else took it like a punch. Mrs Heremaia got hers. One for each son. Dear God, you'd think they could have left her one. Irene Woodhurst walking around for days, dry-eyed and stunned, then finally bursting into tears in Morrisons'. Howling. Embarrassing everybody. Calling Brian's name over and over. And the man behind the counter called her hysterical. She wasn't hysterical. Just . . . cheated.

Then you all started coming home. One by one. Gordon Douglas with no legs. Then Lofty Allen with a hollow in the side of his head where they'd put a metal plate. One by one.

And finally you.

She turns and puts her arms around him, laying her head against his back.

Standing in the sunlight on Orari Station. Looking as strong and perfect as I'd remembered you. I was afraid to believe it. You looked at me and held out your arms and said, 'Elizabeth'. And I ran to you, and it was the first time I'd seen you cry. And I, deceived again, thought the horror was finally over.

Because each night you told me something new. Every night some wound tore open inside you and a wave of blood washed out, drenching us in our bed. And inside each wound was another, deeper one. Macky Heremaia's head splattered across your tunic. Brian Woodhurst going under the tracks of a tank.

He turns and lays his head in her lap, curling up like a child.

You lay in my arms and wept and shook so badly I thought you were dying. I was afraid of sleeping; afraid of the nightmares. I was afraid of you.

She strokes his body gently.

While you were gone my flesh burned for you. I thirsted to have you strong in my arms. Hard inside me. Your body, your laughter, your dreams, your despair, everything you feared, everything you knew. I lusted for it all. And you gave me everything. Nothing was forbidden. I touched it all. Each new horror was proof of your love. I was drowning in it, and I nearly left you because of the biggest deceit of all. I'd thought love would be an easy thing.

A long beat. He sits up, then gets to his feet. He moves away and stands with his back to her. A beat.

Tom   You make me feel deceitful. I wasn't trying to prove anything. I wasn't even thinking of you. I just needed you.

Elizabeth   Tom. That's what makes it real. That's what puts all the trivial things into perspective.

Tom   What trivial things?

Elizabeth   The petty annoyances.

Tom   Annoyances?

Elizabeth   Yes. The little things that grate when you know someone well.

Tom   Grate?

Elizabeth   Yes, Tom. Grate.

Tom   I grate on you?

Elizabeth   Well . . . not so much grate as . . .

Tom   Annoy?

Elizabeth   Sometimes.

Tom   Such as when?

Elizabeth   Such as when . . . well . . . when you blow off in bed.

Tom   What about you? The way you go all tight-lipped and silent when you know you're wrong.

He pushes her.

Elizabeth   I do not.

She pushes him.

Tom   You do.

He pushes her back. She slaps his arm away.

Elizabeth   Well you pick your nose . . .

The pushes turn to grappling, the grappling to wrestling.

Tom   And you always want to know what I'm reading.

Elizabeth   And you scratch your bottom in front of visitors. And you always leave the lid off the toothpaste so it goes crusty.

Tom   At least I don't leave my underwear soaking in the hand basin so nobody can wash their hands, do I.

Elizabeth   Well at least I don't dribble on the toilet seat. Do I!

Tom   And you have that smug way of smacking your lips when you sip your tea.

Elizabeth   What?

Tom   And you never want an ice cream, but then you always want a taste of mine.

Elizabeth   Well what's wrong with that?

She dumps him on the ground and rolls on top of him, arms and legs splayed, pinning him to the ground.

Tom   Aagghh! You big galumph.

She lifts her arms and legs off the ground, then slams them down, bouncing her weight on him. She does it two or three times. He yells in mock terror and pain. He tickles her in the ribs. She squeals and rolls off him. She comes to her knees, pointing at him accusingly.

Elizabeth   You tickled me!

Tom   You galumphed me!

Elizabeth   Tickling's worse than galumphing.

He gets to his feet.

Tom Okay, we're quits. No more galumphing.

Elizabeth Or tickling!

He moves behind her.

Tom Or tickling.

He grabs her from behind, pinning her arms to her sides. They topple sideways to the ground.

Ha ha . . . What are you going to do now, Lizard Breath?

She twists her head around and nuzzles him lovingly on the cheek . . . then bites his ear hard. He yells, and lets her go. She grabs him by the nose and stands. He is on his knees in front of her. He speaks nasally.

Ah . . . I see. That old trick. Very effective. Well done. Okay, we're really quits now.

A beat.

Elizabeth?

Elizabeth No more tickling?

Tom Absolutely. No more tickling.

Elizabeth And no more calling me 'Lizard Breath'?

A beat. She tightens her grip and twists his nose a bit. He flinches.

Tom Agh! All right, all right. No more calling you . . . you know what. Elizabeth.

Elizabeth Promise?

Tom Absolutely.

She releases him. He jumps to his feet and whips out his crossed fingers from behind his back.

. . . not!

He laughs and does an exaggerated dumb show of picking his nose. He strolls back to the tub, scratching his bottom in the same way. He picks up the knife and an apple. She has gone tight-lipped and silent. He returns, pointedly clamping his lips tightly together. She self-consciously relaxes hers.

He slices a piece off the apple and puts it in his mouth, then licks the knife blade. He chews, all the time looking at her with a teasing arrogance. She returns his gaze steadily, accepting the challenge, with a faint trace of amusement. He slices off another piece of apple, puts it in his mouth, and again lifts the blade to his tongue.

She shoots out her hand and grasps his wrist. She pulls the knife to her mouth and licks the juice off the blade.

He turns the knife, and she runs her tongue along the sharp edge. He points the knife at her. She puts her mouth over it and closes her lips on the blade, her gaze never leaving his. There is the sound of a blade scraping on metal, and the following moves are accompanied by tense musical sounds. Both their faces show an amused challenge.

He lightly slashes the knife to one side, then the other, but she moves in perfect synergy, anticipating his moves. Suddenly he stabs forward. She is taken by surprise, but still manages to ride the move. The smile fades from both their faces. He slashes a couple more times, then draws the knife out of her mouth, as letting her off the hook.

He lowers the blade, smiling, and takes another slice of apple, grinning at her, but she grabs his wrist again, and replaces it in her mouth, eyeing him defiantly. There is the blade-on-metal sound again, and the music.

Tom   All right, then.

He begins slashing and stabbing again, more vicious and prolonged than before. She stumbles but keeps her balance. Finally, she is forced down on to the ground, on her back, knees crooked up. Her head touches the ground and they stare at each other. The music stops.

He draws the knife out of her mouth; we hear it scrape on her teeth. He lays it on her chest and kneels down beside her. He strokes her leg, sliding her dress up.

Tom   We know each other too well.

She takes the knife and draws its tip lightly down his forehead, balancing its point momentarily against his eyeball. He is relaxed, trusting. She draws it down his cheek, throat, chest, stomach and groin . . .

Elizabeth   Did you know I had a lover?

. . . and she plunges the knife into his stomach; a double thrust. There is the crack of thunder. He doubles over, gasping, clutching his stomach, and crawls groaning towards the tub.

I thought not.

He is leaning over the tub, coughing and lifting handfuls of water to his stomach.

Oh come on. It's only a flesh wound.

A beat.

Tom?

Tom   It hurts!

Elizabeth   Don't be pathetic. It was long ago. During the war. You were away.

He is on his feet now.

Tom   Who was it?

Elizabeth   He was –

Tom   Don't tell me!

A beat.

Who was it?

Elizabeth   A shearer.

Tom   A shearer?! What kind of shearer?

Elizabeth   A sheep shearer! How many kinds of shearer are there?!

Tom   I mean what kind of a man was he?

Elizabeth   A boy.

Tom   Did he force himself on you?

A faintly scornful reaction from her.

You should have told me. I would've understood.

Elizabeth   You'd've reacted badly.

Tom (*reacting badly*)   I would not have reacted badly!

She looks at him, making a silent point. He lowers his glare.

Elizabeth   And he didn't force himself on me. He was young, and smooth-cheeked, and uncertain. And I seduced him.

Tom   You betrayed me.

Elizabeth   Yes, I betrayed you.

Tom   Why?

Elizabeth   Because I wanted to see if I could live for just one second without thinking about you! I wanted to know that I could survive! That I could forget you if I had to! I wanted to kill you so they couldn't take you away from me!

Tom   Well couldn't you have just got into a good book or something?

Elizabeth   I think I needed something a bit more potent than that!

Tom   And he was 'potent', was he?

Elizabeth   He –

Tom   Don't tell me!

A long beat.

So did you?

Elizabeth   Did I what?

Tom   Forget me.

Elizabeth   No. I didn't. Even at the very moment of . . .

He winces.

Elizabeth   . . . there was your face. But it was all right, because at least I knew. I knew who I was and how things were. It was rather a comfort.

Tom   Why are you telling me now?

Elizabeth   Because I'm going soon, and that was my second to last secret.

She walks back to the tub and kneels beside it. He thinks about what she has just said, and makes a show of not asking the obvious question. Then his face changes as if he has remembered something. He turns away from her, thinking, and squats, staring out.

A long beat.

Tom   Looks like rain.

She stares at him. Soft music begins, a haunting, Celtic-sounding melody.

Elizabeth   There was a boarding house in Cairo, in a district called the Berka. And on a second-floor landing, a line of soldiers stood outside a closed door. And each soldier had a handful of coins, or a gift. Stockings. Perfume. And every few minutes –

Tom   Every few minutes the door would open and a soldier would come out and the next would go in. And a few minutes later he would come out, without his money, or his gift. And one young soldier came out with tears drying on his face, because he was young, and he believed he was going to die, and because the woman in the room had smelled of cinnamon.

A long beat. The music fades. She gently sings the same melody.

Elizabeth   Come tell me all you brave young men,
    Wide rivers across the plains.
    When will I see my love again?
    Wide rivers roll . . .

*She hums the tune softly to herself idly swirling the water in the tub
with her hand. Slowly he gets up and walks to the tub. He kneels
opposite her, but doesn't catch her eye. She looks at him, then lifts her
hand and flicks water into his face. He looks at her. She does it
again, this time with a flicker of a smile. She raises a handful of
water to her mouth, then looks at him with a slightly mischievous
expression. Suddenly she spits the water into his face.*

*A beat. They both dip their faces in the water, draw in a mouthful,
and kneel, facing each other.*

*A beat, then simultaneously they spit water at each other. They move
to embrace, but she has some left, and as their faces draw close, she
spits again. He recoils, she giggles. They move to embrace, and he
spits the remainder of his. They burst into laughter, hugging each
other, falling sideways to the ground, her on top. The laughter and
hugging turns to a deep, sensual kiss. They draw their faces apart.*

Tom   Remember our hay barn?

Elizabeth   I remember everything. What made you think
of that?

Tom   I'm just remembering how good you looked with
straw in your hair.

Elizabeth   Oh. That. It had its moments. One particularly
memorable one.

Tom   Which was that?

Elizabeth   One day when we were . . . playing in the hay,
and you started to . . .

Tom   What? What'd I start to do?

Elizabeth   Well . . . tickle my bottom. And I thought, 'Ooh,
Tom. This is new . . .' and I started to . . . respond – you
know. And the tickling got more . . . insistent. . . and I
suddenly realised I could see both your hands.

They laugh and roll apart.

Tom   And you let out an almighty scream and were out the door in one leap.

Elizabeth   Do you blame me?

Tom   Leaving behind the flattest-looking field mouse I've ever seen.

Their laughter continues.

But boy, did he ever have a big smile on his face!

Their laughter increases then subsides.

Elizabeth   I miss the farm so much.

Tom   We've got mice here.

She swipes at him playfully.

Elizabeth   You know what I mean.

A beat.

You do too, don't you.

A beat.

Don't you.

Tom   It was a big part of me. Of both of us. While I was overseas it was like an anchor. The still point in all the chaos.

He gets to his feet. Moves around. She is lying on her stomach, listening to him.

Not just our farm, but this whole place. The plains. The Southern Alps. Names used to roll through my head like some kind of litany. Geraldine. Pleasant Point. Fairlie. Little nothing names full of magic. Up through Burke's Pass to the big lakes. Tekapo. Pukaki. And the rivers. The Waitaki. The Rangitata. And the big Rakaia churning milky and rich through the gorge. Names that seemed to invoke something vast. That recalled me to who I was and where I belonged.

I knew when I came home it would be time to take the
farm. Mum and Dad were ready to move into town. They
were old.

He sits astride her back, strokes her hair and shoulders.

I remember that day on Orari Station. I was afraid to believe
it too. I felt shattered. I hadn't slept. When you ran into my
arms, I thought at any moment I would wake up, back in the
desert, with the dream fading like sand through my fingers.
For a few days we stepped carefully round each other,
remember? Getting to know ourselves again. Gently feeling
out the familiar things in each other.

He gets off and kneels beside her. She touches him as he speaks.

Then we moved on to the farm. There's something about
the land. Something about belonging to it, sharing its
history. Seeing the kids cutting across the far paddock to the
willows for a swim after school, the same way we used to.
Hearing the magpies in the pines of a morning, down the
end of the house paddock.

Elizabeth   Dive-bombing me when I went to hang the
washing out.

Tom   The river with its wide shingle bed, bringing down
that rich alluvial mix from the Alps. It was fine land. You
could crumble it in your fingers. Dig your toes into it. You
could almost feel it humming with life. Good, wide, sunlit
country. Somewhere a man could set his ghosts free.

*He fetches a bucket, places it upside down on the floor and sits on it.
She swings her legs up on to his lap.*

There's a picture I have. I was fencing one time, way up the
back in one of the river paddocks. A hot day. And you
walked all the way out to bring me some food. I saw you
coming in the distance. The mountains were close that day,
and the sun dazzled off the river. And you, walking with
your dress hitched up, bringing us a picnic.

He looks at her, stroking her legs. He sings, the same melody.

> I saw my love in golden light,
> Wide rivers across the plains.
> Beyond her rose the mountains white,
> Wide rivers roll.

She joins him in the song.

Both   And we will walk on shingle sand,
> Wide rivers across the plains.
> Again I'll hold my true love's hand,

He stops singing.

Elizabeth   Wide rivers roll.

He looks thoughtful. A beat.

Elizabeth   What's the matter?

She nudges him with her foot.

Tom?

He eases her legs off his lap, stands, moves away.

Tom   Who owns it now, eh? The bank!

Elizabeth   We did what we could, love. Some years were hard. Hard for everyone.

Tom   Midwinter. You'd gone off early to some Women's Institute thing. I went out to the kennels to let the dogs off, crunching the frost. I could hardly undo their chains. There was pain in my knuckles. They looked swollen and grey with age. Just the cold, I thought. Then I went to the shed and tried to pull back the door bolt. The pain was awful. It made my arms go numb. I tried for quarter of an hour to shift that bolt. I never budged it an inch.

So I started to walk. Around the farm. The dogs looked at me as if to say, 'What's goin' on, boss? This isn't what we're supposed to be doin'!' We walked all day. The house paddock, the willows, the pines, the river paddocks – all of it.

Got back to the house late afternoon, my hands still throbbing. The day had never properly warmed up.

And I couldn't get into the house. I couldn't open the door. I sat down on the step, and the dogs seemed to know what was happening. They lay down either side, pressed close. And we sat there. Three old boys, waiting for you to come home.

Elizabeth Yes. There you were. My old grey tomcat and his mates. But it was all right, wasn't it? It had been a good run. We'd done all right.

Tom We had, hadn't we.

A long beat.

Elizabeth Will you wash my hair?

Tom Does it need it?

Elizabeth Not really.

She grins at him. He smiles back.

Tom Okay. Come on.

She lies against the tub, propped on her elbows, with her head tipped back over the lip. Her attitude shows this is something she enjoys. He kneels on the other side of the tub, and lifts handfuls of water, letting them run through her hair. This continues in silence for a few seconds.

Tom How's that?

Elizabeth Mmm.

A beat. The sound of water.

Will you wash my body when I'm dead?

Tom Elizabeth!

Elizabeth It's going to happen.

Tom Well we needn't talk about it.

A beat.

Elizabeth   But will you?

Tom   Yes, I'll wash you.

Elizabeth   Not me. My body. I'll be gone. Flying with the magpies. Once around the farm for a last look, then away.

Tom   Where to?

A beat.

Elizabeth   Somewhere only magpies know about.

Tom   Oh. Oamaru!

They laugh. A beat.

Elizabeth   Only I don't want some ghastly old undertaker putting his clammy fingers on me.

Tom   It's their job. They're used to it.

Elizabeth   Well I'm not.

Tom   It won't be you. You'll be gone.

Elizabeth   But what if I mess my pants or something? I don't want anyone else to see. The thought of it!

During the next few lines she becomes increasingly aroused by his touch and the water running through her hair. She writhes her legs slightly, stroking her thigh with one hand, clenching a fistful of dress.

And you'll have to tidy up the room, too . . .
put some fresh flowers in the vase on the windowsill . . .
open the window so the scent is wafted into the room . . .
and lay me in clean sheets . . .
Ohh . . . that feels so good. . .

His head is bent over her. She reaches up, lifts her face to his, pulls him down to her, and they kiss.

Elizabeth   Have we ever done it in the bath?

Tom   The bath? Let me think.

A short beat.

We've done it in the river.

Elizabeth   And on the bank.

Tom   Was that you?

Elizabeth   Were you exhausted?

Tom   Totally.

Elizabeth   It was me.

Laughter. The hair-washing continues.

Elizabeth   That's wonderful.

Tom   Kitty used to love it when I washed her hair like this, too.

Her expression hardens. He continues . . .

Poor Kitty.

She sits up and begins to squeeze the water out of her hair.

What's the matter?

Elizabeth   'Poor Kitty!'

Tom   Well?

A beat.

I don't see –

Elizabeth   No, you never do, do you!

Tom   What's that supposed to mean?

She walks away. He moves angrily after her and grabs her by the wrist, hard.

Tom   What do you mean?!

She jerks her arm, but he keeps his grip. They stand still, eye to eye. She glances down at her wrist then back at him. He opens his hand, but she leaves her wrist against his palm for a defiant beat, then lifts it away. The moment passes.

Elizabeth   She's not coming, is she.

Tom   No. She's not.

Elizabeth   You told her everything?

Tom   Everything.

A beat.

It's hard for her.

Elizabeth   It's hard for me. How long are you going to use that excuse?

Tom   For as long as it's true!

Elizabeth   You always take her side! I'm forever outnumbered!

Tom   It's not a matter of sides or numbers!

Elizabeth   I always knew it would turn out like this!

Tom   Maybe if you hadn't been so convinced of that, things would've been different.

Elizabeth   I was trying to be sensible, that's all. Realistic. Instead, I'm some kind of monster!

Tom   That's not true.

Elizabeth   . . . while you're so kind and supportive. You have her confidences. And you tell me it's not a matter of sides! I wish you knew how it feels!

Tom   I know how it feels to love somebody.

Elizabeth *makes a short scoffing sound.*

Tom   I know what it's like to have your parents say, 'She's not the one for you. Her family aren't educated or well off. She knows you have a farm coming to you. Knows you have connections. That's what she really wants. You can do a lot better than her.'

And you tell them you love her, and they say, 'What do you know about love?' And you hear it again and again until you start to doubt. You really start to doubt. And then you go to her, and you feel that as long as she's with you, you can move the world.

But that chill of disapproval always lurks. It taints and weakens everything. Takes a long time to go away. I swore I'd never make anyone feel like that. I wanted Kitty to know that we didn't love her any less for her choice.

Elizabeth   She breaks my heart.

Tom   And you break hers. She thinks you sit in judgement on her.

Elizabeth   'It's been seven years now. There's just me and the baby. London is hell. I don't want to die an old woman.'

Tom   What's that?

Elizabeth   The last message Kitty sent me. A card.

Tom   I don't remember it.

Elizabeth   It was addressed to me. It felt like a punishment. 'See? It all happened just like you said it would. I'm alone and miserable. Happy now?' I'm her mother, and I don't even know who she is.

Tom   When I called her, she asked me to tell you that she loves you.

Elizabeth   Did she?

A long beat. They look at each other.

Tom   Elizabeth . . . we're not perfect. We're not immortal. We struggle and we do what we can. And that's enough.

Silence. He sits beside her. They don't speak or touch or look at each other, but their body language joins them. A long beat.

Elizabeth   What time is it?

Tom   Just past noon.

She rises.

Elizabeth   It's a fine hot day. A good day for leaving.

Tom   Is there such a thing?

Elizabeth   Have you tidied the room?

Tom   Yes.

She brightens.

Elizabeth   I wish I could see the farm.

Tom   You can imagine how it is.

Elizabeth   Mmm. I can smell the pines. I can see the Alps straggling across the horizon. I can even feel the cool shade under the willows by the swimming hole.

Tom   That's just how it'll be.

A beat. She looks at him.

Elizabeth   Have you put fresh flowers in the vase?

Tom   Yes.

A beat.

Elizabeth   If this bed could speak, what tales it would tell.

Tom   Perhaps we're lucky it can't.

She kneels on the mats, smiling.

Elizabeth   There was a time, not too long ago, we'd sometimes spend our whole day in it.

I remember lying in it with Kitty in my arms. A little red, wrinkled bundle, nuzzling at my breast.

She lightly touches one breast with her fingertips. She lowers her hands and rests them briefly over her womb. A look of pain passes quickly over her face.

And now I can't get up even if I wanted to.

A long beat. She rises to her feet. She looks at him.

Have you opened the window?

Tom   Yes.

Elizabeth   I'm not afraid, Tom. Sooner or later your life becomes parched. Its rivers run thin. Its mountains have melted into the distance as blue and cool as memories. It gathers its cracked old skin and peers thirstily at the wall of black thunderheads coming from the south. Just wants to lie in the dark and feel the rain.

I've given all the crops I can. Had all the sun I can take. I want to stand naked in the rain. Open my pores and drink it in. Feel my skin tighten across my body, uncrinkling, softening. My back will uncurl, my limbs become long and clean. And I'll stretch up into that beautiful water, and I'll look the way I really am.

Tom   The way I see you.

She smiles at him. It fades. He goes to her, puts his arms around her.

What's the matter?

Elizabeth   It's a lie. This is the best of all possible worlds, and I don't want to leave.

He backs away from her, drawing her arm out, until their fingers part and her arm falls. He smiles at her, almost cheekily and offers his hand. She smiles back and takes it. Soft old-time waltz music plays as they draw together and dance.

Elizabeth   What do you feel for me, my old grey tomcat?

Tom   Passion.

Elizabeth   Are you going to let me go?

Tom   Not without a fight.

Elizabeth   It's a waste.

Tom   It's mine to waste.

Elizabeth   It's futile.

Tom   Then it's pure.

The waltz music segues into a sensual, rhythmic piece as they kiss and he lowers her gracefully on to her back on the floor.

They begin to make love. The first few seconds consist of exactly the same moves as the first few seconds of the opening fight, but this time they are played sensuously and erotically instead of violently.

Rather than literally portraying a couple having sex, their moves indicate joy, desperation, passion, self indulgence, obsession with each other, and absolute physical abandonment. The music, and their movements, become increasingly wild, frantic and erotic. This is that 'last mad, sad fuck'.

As the sequence approaches a climax, they cling together, spinning, kissing desperately and passionately. There is a huge clap of thunder and they are flung apart. He is thrown to the floor near a front corner of the mats. She stays on her feet, near the corner diagonally opposite. He reaches to her. She is out of reach.

The thunder rolls into silence, except for the sound of soft rain falling. She lifts her face into the rain, then begins to unbutton her dress. Over the rain, music begins – the melody of the song they have sung.

He gets to his feet and also undresses as he is trying to go with her. They stand naked, statue-like, for a moment, then she moves to the tub and kneels alongside it in profile to the audience. She reaches up to him; he takes her hand and kneels opposite her, their knees touching.

The music is becoming louder and richer. They bend toward each other as if they are going to kiss, but instead they nuzzle each other, foreheads, cheeks, faces. While they do this they each take a turn rising up on to their knees so that for few moments each in turn is above the other.

They kneel up together, and embrace tightly. Loosening the embrace, he reaches down and lifts the cloth from the tub. Holding it at arm's length above her he squeezes the water from it. She arches backwards, the water splashing over her throat and chest. She slides her hands up his thighs, torso and arms, and takes the cloth. She presses it against his chest, then his back, squeezing water over him.

She throws the cloth into the tub, hard enough to make a splash. They kneel down, and he gently flicks water over her from the tub. She does the same to him, a little harder. He smiles and does it again, harder still, until they are both laughing and splashing furiously, giggling like children, sending sheets of water over each other, making their bodies slick.

They leap to their feet, still laughing and embrace tightly, slowly turning around. The music is now loud, rich and grand. Their laughter turns to weeping.

They draw their faces apart and, still clinging to each other, they speak, but their voices are inaudible under the music. This is their last intimacy, and we are excluded.

Elizabeth   I have to go.

Tom   I know.

Elizabeth   I don't want to leave.

Tom   We'll be all right, love. We'll be all right.

Elizabeth   Tom. I remember everything.

The music is slowly fading. He carefully helps her into the tub. Her head is arched back over one end. Her arms are outside the tub, lying forward along the floor. Her knees are bent over the other end of the tub, feet on the floor. She is dead.

He moves behind the tub, and kneels beside it. The music has faded to silence. He looks at her for a beat, then begins to sing softly, gently washing her body.

Tom   I saw my love in golden light
  Wide rivers across the plains.
  Beyond her rose the mountains white,
  Wide rivers roll.
  And we will walk on shingle sand
  Wide rivers across the plains.
  Again I'll hold my true love's hand . . .

He presses her hand to his face and weeps. After a few moments he becomes silent and motionless in that position.

Beyond the tub, a very old man walks forward out of the gloom. He stops, barely registering the tableau in front of him. He is dressed in a singlet and brown woollen trousers held up with braces. He is barefoot and carries an apple and a knife. He slices into the apple with the knife. There comes the ringing call of magpies. The old man pauses and stares up into the sky. He stands motionless, as the call rings out again, and the lights fade to black. In the darkness the magpies' cry segues into the end music.

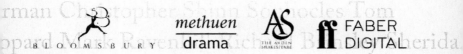

Bloomsbury Methuen Drama Modern Plays

include work by

Bola Agbaje	Robert Holman
Edward Albee	Caroline Horton
Davey Anderson	Terry Johnson
Jean Anouilh	Sarah Kane
John Arden	Barrie Keeffe
Peter Barnes	Doug Lucie
Sebastian Barry	Anders Lustgarten
Alistair Beaton	David Mamet
Brendan Behan	Patrick Marber
Edward Bond	Martin McDonagh
William Boyd	Arthur Miller
Bertolt Brecht	D. C. Moore
Howard Brenton	Tom Murphy
Amelia Bullmore	Phyllis Nagy
Anthony Burgess	Anthony Neilson
Leo Butler	Peter Nichols
Jim Cartwright	Joe Orton
Lolita Chakrabarti	Joe Penhall
Caryl Churchill	Luigi Pirandello
Lucinda Coxon	Stephen Poliakoff
Curious Directive	Lucy Prebble
Nick Darke	Peter Quilter
Shelagh Delaney	Mark Ravenhill
Ishy Din	Philip Ridley
Claire Dowie	Willy Russell
David Edgar	Jean-Paul Sartre
David Eldridge	Sam Shepard
Dario Fo	Martin Sherman
Michael Frayn	Wole Soyinka
John Godber	Simon Stephens
Paul Godfrey	Peter Straughan
James Graham	Kate Tempest
David Greig	Theatre Workshop
John Guare	Judy Upton
Mark Haddon	Timberlake Wertenbaker
Peter Handke	Roy Williams
David Harrower	Snoo Wilson
Jonathan Harvey	Frances Ya-Chu Cowhig
Iain Heggie	Benjamin Zephaniah

Bloomsbury Methuen Drama Contemporary Dramatists

include

John Arden (two volumes)
Arden & D'Arcy
Peter Barnes (three volumes)
Sebastian Barry
Mike Bartlett
Dermot Bolger
Edward Bond (eight volumes)
Howard Brenton (two volumes)
Leo Butler
Richard Cameron
Jim Cartwright
Caryl Churchill (two volumes)
Complicite
Sarah Daniels (two volumes)
Nick Darke
David Edgar (three volumes)
David Eldridge (two volumes)
Ben Elton
Per Olov Enquist
Dario Fo (two volumes)
Michael Frayn (four volumes)
John Godber (four volumes)
Paul Godfrey
James Graham
David Greig
John Guare
Lee Hall (two volumes)
Katori Hall
Peter Handke
Jonathan Harvey (two volumes)
Iain Heggie
Israel Horovitz
Declan Hughes
Terry Johnson (three volumes)
Sarah Kane
Barrie Keeffe
Bernard-Marie Koltès (two volumes)
Franz Xaver Kroetz
Kwame Kwei-Armah
David Lan
Bryony Lavery
Deborah Levy
Doug Lucie

David Mamet (four volumes)
Patrick Marber
Martin McDonagh
Duncan McLean
David Mercer (two volumes)
Anthony Minghella (two volumes)
Tom Murphy (six volumes)
Phyllis Nagy
Anthony Neilson (two volumes)
Peter Nichol (two volumes)
Philip Osment
Gary Owen
Louise Page
Stewart Parker (two volumes)
Joe Penhall (two volumes)
Stephen Poliakoff (three volumes)
David Rabe (two volumes)
Mark Ravenhill (three volumes)
Christina Reid
Philip Ridley (two volumes)
Willy Russell
Eric-Emmanuel Schmitt
Ntozake Shange
Sam Shepard (two volumes)
Martin Sherman (two volumes)
Christopher Shinn
Joshua Sobel
Wole Soyinka (two volumes)
Simon Stephens (three volumes)
Shelagh Stephenson
David Storey (three volumes)
C. P. Taylor
Sue Townsend
Judy Upton
Michel Vinaver (two volumes)
Arnold Wesker (two volumes)
Peter Whelan
Michael Wilcox
Roy Williams (four volumes)
David Williamson
Snoo Wilson (two volumes)
David Wood (two volumes)
Victoria Wood

For a complete catalogue
of Bloomsbury Methuen Drama
titles write to:

Bloomsbury Methuen Drama
Bloomsbury Publishing Plc
50 Bedford Square
London WC1B 3DP

or you can visit our website at:
www.bloomsbury.com/drama